ossia 8va
ff
f
ff
colla parte
sempre f
ossia 8va bassa
ff
p
pp sub.
pp
cant.
pp
morendo

T0087055

Poco animato
appass.
f
fp
p
p
f
f
cantabile
f
dim.
p

R. Vaughan Williams

ROMANCE for Viola and Piano

Oxford University Press

ROMANCE

for Viola and Piano

The viola part edited by Bernard Shore
The piano part edited by Eric Gritton

R. VAUGHAN WILLIAMS

There is no information about the approximate date on which this work was written. The manuscript was discovered with others, without any clue, among the composer's papers after his death. All that can be said is that it was probably intended for the great virtuoso Lionel Tertis, for whom Vaughan Williams had composed his two major works for the viola – *Flos Campi* in 1925 and the Suite in 1934.

Bernard Shore

A separate viola part is included with this score

This work was first performed by Bernard Shore and Eric Gritton in a Macnaghten Concert on 19 January 1962

© Oxford University Press 1962

Printed in Great Britain
OXFORD UNIVERSITY PRESS, MUSIC DEPARTMENT, GREAT CLARENDON STREET, OXFORD OX2 6DP

Photocopying this copyright material is ILLEGAL.

Viola

ROMANCE

for Viola and Piano

Edited by Bernard Shore

R. VAUGHAN WILLIAMS

There is no information about the approximate date on which this work was written. The manuscript was discovered with others, without any clue, among the composer's papers after his death. All that can be said is that it was probably intended for the great virtuoso Lionel Tertis, for whom Vaughan Williams had composed his two major works for the viola—*Flos Campi* in 1925 and the Suite in 1934.

Bernard Shore

This work was first performed by Bernard Shore and Eric Gritton in a Macnaghten Concert on 19 January 1962

© Oxford University Press 1962

Printed in Great Britain

OXFORD UNIVERSITY PRESS, MUSIC DEPARTMENT, GREAT CLARENDON STREET, OXFORD OX2 6DP

Photocopying this copyright material is ILLEGAL.

OXFORD UNIVERSITY PRESS

f
f cantabile
colla parte
f cantabile
Largamente
ff
Largamente
ff
f
meno f
con Ped.
Tempo I
pp
p
pp sostenuto

ppp una corda
cant.
tre corde
poco a poco cresc.
cant.
poco a poco cresc.
f
mf
dim.

slent.
Con sord.
pp
slent.
più p
pp una corda al fine
dolciss.
mf
poco sf
p
(pp)
ppp
ppp

OXFORD MUSIC FOR VIOLA includes:

Bach *arr. Forbes*	Sheep may safely graze
arr. Forbes	A first year classical album A second year classical album Baroque Pieces Classical and Romantic Pieces Popular Pieces Tunes and Dances
Handel *arr. Forbes*	The arrival of the Queen of Sheba Sonata in G
Mackay	Easy position tunes A modern viola method
Murray and Tate	The New Viola Books, Book 2
Vaughan Williams	Romance

ISBN 978-0-19-359271-1

OXFORD UNIVERSITY PRESS